I0177479

Recollections of Life in a Siberian Labor Camp

A Personal Memoir by Halina Jaworski

Copyright © 2020 Double J Publishing LLC

Recollections of Life in a Siberian Labor Camp
A Personal Memoir by Halina Jaworski
All Rights Reserved

No part of this publication may be reproduced, distributed, or transmitted in any form or by any means, including photocopying, recording, or other electronic or mechanical methods, without the prior written permission of the publisher, except in the case of brief quotations embodied in critical reviews and other non-commercial uses permitted by copyright law.

This book is a memoir and reflects the author's experiences over time. Although the events in this book are factual, some names have been changed to protect their identities and the privacy of their families. Some events may have been compressed and some dialogue recreated. Any perceived slight of any individual or organization is purely unintentional. Neither the author nor the publisher assumes any responsibility or liability whatsoever on behalf of the consumer or reader of this material.

ISBN 978-1-7350630-0-3

Double J Publishing LLC
7457 South County Road S Lake Nebagamon, WI 54849
(218) 355-8815

This memoir is dedicated with love to my late husband and present family, and also to my grandmother, father, mother, brother, and sister.

My homeland, you are like the breath of life; how much you should be cherished will only be realized by those who have lost you. (Mickiewicz, *Pan Tadeusz,* 1834)

Acknowledgements

I would like to acknowledge the initial and strong inspiration from my son Thomas who gave me the will and desire to start and accomplish this project.

I wish to also gratefully acknowledge my son Richard for supplying me with the computer to write this memoir, for formatting and editing the text and photographs, for designing the drawings and supplying the map, and for making suggestions for improvements wherever they were needed. I am very grateful for your diligent support by saying, "just keep writing". And so I did, until the end.

Thank you to both of them.

My family at the start of the war

Konstanty Skowronski - Father

Anna Skowronska - Mother

Ryszard Skowronski - Brother

Elwira Skowronska – Sister

Halina Jaworski (Skowronska)

Zofia Sciblo – Grandmother
The only remaining picture.
Her grave in Tehran.

Introduction

I was born in the eastern part of Poland and my family and I lived there until the first part of World War II. I had just turned 13 when on September 1ˢᵗ of 1939 Germany attacked and invaded Poland. This changed the course of my life forever. Soon the first sounds of German planes were heard above our heads. It did not take them long to reach the extreme eastern part of Poland. The bombardments over us were quite frequent and frightening. My father, seeing how panic stricken we were every time the bombardment began was looking for an opportunity to get us farther east where my uncle lived. This materialized when a refugee from central Poland, trying to escape the Germans, came to our house. His car was running out of gas and he was unable to get a refill. My father offered to help him, and in return he promised to take the four of us; my mother, brother, sister, and myself all the way east toward the Soviet border to my uncle's place. In his opinion, the farther east we could go, the safer we would be.

My father and grandmother stayed behind. We arrived at my uncle's safely and only had to get out of the car and hide in a ditch once. German planes were flying low over the road and shooting at whoever was in sight. Within a few days however we found out that it was not to be a safe refuge. On September 17, 1939 we heard on the radio that the Soviet Army had crossed our border and was proceeding west into our country.

This was done without any warning and in a secret agreement with the Germans. My uncle did not think that it was safe for us to stay, so we packed and proceeded west to find refuge in the city of Pinsk. The Soviet Army was still behind us; there were some battles with the remnants of the Polish Army and they continued outside the city limits of Pinsk. We were staying at a hotel and heard the artillery fire throughout the night. This was my first very frightening experience of the fierce battle of war. It was happening over the city and very close to us. I was very young and this was the first time I felt terrified and helpless.

Within a day or two, the Soviets took over the city and we were under their occupation. My mother decided that we should try to get back to our home in Antopol. Why stay in the hotel if the Soviets are everywhere anyway? The stay was expensive. My uncle secured train tickets for us to get back home.

Back home we found out that my father was arrested, presumably for his own safety from local "unfriendly factions" and was kept in a local school by armed "officials". Upon hearing rumors that he was to be taken out and shot at night, my mother went there and pleaded with the guards on her knees and bribed them with her engagement ring. She managed to get the guards to agree to set him free and she brought him back home. My father did not feel safe there anymore so we took refuge in the city of Kobryn, a nearby larger city and settled in a small apartment. My grandmother stayed behind. She was not afraid for herself. Later on, my uncle and his wife joined us and roomed in the apartment next door.

Things had changed rapidly under the Soviet regime. The stores were being closed, long lines for bread were forming, and there was not much of anything one could get. The three of us children went back to high school which was now controlled by the communist regime. Everything was suddenly in Russian with no trace of the Polish language anywhere. It felt like being in a foreign country. Communist propaganda infiltrated our society and took over our education. However, things seemed to become "normal", and life went on.

An Unexpected Destiny

Suddenly, my life, the lives of my family, and the lives of about 1,500,000 Poles changed completely, forever. A horror story unfolded for all Poles living in the eastern part of Poland at the start of World War II. On February 10, 1940, in the early morning hours before dawn, we were awakened by pounding on our door. My father went to check what was happening. He opened the door and was confronted by three armed Soviet soldiers. They forced themselves in and yelled to my father, "Hands up"!

We were told to get up and get dressed quickly. My father was ordered to sit in a chair with his hands on the table and not to move. My mother was to get as much of our personal clothing as she could and some food within half an hour. One soldier suggested winter clothing mostly because he said it will be cold where we were going. We were being deported they said. We were sitting around the table watching numbly as the soldiers were searching our apartment for military equipment and upon finding my brother's trumpet, they confiscated it, as well as some coins in our change box. I could see that my mother was at a loss about packing our belongings. My brother was more composed and he just shoved whatever clothing was around into some bedding and bundled it up into a sack. They would not allow us to take anything that belonged to my father. This did not register in my mind then, but later it became obvious why. It was all according to their plans.

After about a half an hour, we were ordered to move out, load our belongings on a sled pulled by a horse, and they took us to the train station. There was a long freight train standing on the tracks and many people like us were being pushed into the cars of the train. We were also ordered to get in and take up an assigned place.

The inside of the train car was divided into two parts. Each part had four plain wooden decks, two upper and two lower decks. My family was assigned to the upper deck. There was not very much head room. It was hard to sit up. Our car was being filled up to capacity. More and more people were being brought in throughout the whole day. We were not aware of it at that time, but this was happening to Polish people all along the eastern part of our country. The first night came, my legs were hurting badly, so called "growing pains", and my father was massaging them. Finally, tired and overwhelmed by the depressing events of that fateful day, I fell asleep.

Our sleep was interrupted by the previously barred heavy door being opened and we heard soldiers shouting "Konstanty Skowronski!" That was my father's name. We rose up panic stricken. They ordered him to get up and follow them. We cried bitterly as he was hugging us quickly and saying goodbye. He said, "I don't think I will be seeing you ever again." People were trying to console us saying that they probably just took him for some kind of interrogation and would bring him back by morning.

People were continually being brought to the train. We were occupying the upper deck of our car and this was the same level as the little window of the car. I just could not give up hope of seeing my father so I kept looking for him, peering through the small bars. Suddenly I saw someone trying to get through the line of armed soldiers guarding our train. The soldiers would not let him cross the line so he stopped and looked at the train. I recognized this handsome man immediately. It was my dear uncle. He came to see us so he just stood there, clearly very upset. As I watched, I saw him pull out his handkerchief and wipe his eyes. Then he turned and walked away. To this day I have the picture of my dear uncle in my memory. Standing there hopelessly and helplessly and holding his handkerchief close to his face. I never saw him again. Unfortunately, my father's words were prophetic as well. He did not come back either. We never did see him again. He was 41 years old and removed from our lives.

The soldiers brought my grandmother however. I could hear her voice as two armed soldiers were escorting her, and she was loudly putting them to shame that they needed two armed soldiers to escort a 72-year-old woman. As they pushed her up into our car, she turned around and said, pointing her finger at them, "I will be back and I will teach you a lesson!" That was my grandmother, never afraid to speak up. I felt comforted to see her joining us. From there on, she was to be my stronghold, my shield in all the brutal events that were facing me. By midmorning evidently, the train was filled to capacity and began to move. It was headed east and moving fast. I could see despair showing on faces around me. Going east meant only one thing. We were being deported to Siberia. I looked around and sadly noticed that all families were complete, only mine lacked the presence of a very important person in my life. My father was missing. I felt like I was orphaned. My 17-year-old brother was the only male in my family of five now. People were trying to calm us saying that maybe they put him on the train but in a different car and we will be reunited when we get to wherever we are destined to be. I clung to that hope for the duration. The train stopped at the Soviet border for a moment as if to give us a memento, "Say goodbye to your country and your past life." We began to cry aloud. My brother began to sing a favorite patriotic/religious hymn and all joined him. This was a good thing to do. It gave us a little strength and hope.

The train was moving very fast now stopping for a short while only on secluded tracks to let us get out for a moment. We were being watched by armed soldiers who were yelling for us to be quick. I felt subhuman and embarrassed. We were moving east at first and then turned north. On the way, when we stopped in secluded small rural areas we could see women and children running toward our train with their outstretched arms crying and begging for bread, oblivious of the soldiers around our train. This was a shocking revelation for me. If these people, free Soviet citizens are begging us for food, then what will happen to us, the prisoners?

It was hard to measure time but I think that after about two weeks the train stopped and unloaded part of our train in the back and a few days later it stopped to make us get out with all our belongings. A small depot surrounded by vast forests as far as I could see. I looked around in desperation at people getting out searching for my father, but there was no sign of him. I cried in vain, feeling abandoned like an orphan. What have they done to him? And why? My wonderful daddy, popular, liked and respected by all law-abiding citizens. What could they have against him? What could they charge him with? With a heavy heart I began to follow the long and pitiful caravan of people moving toward their unknown destiny.

The armed soldiers stayed on the train. They were not needed to guard us anymore. Where would we go? What were we to do except follow the horse drawn sleds driven by Ukrainian men? Small children and old people could ride on the sleds. The rest of us walked. The drivers were rather friendly and looking around at our rather large group. They were saying that we were lucky. At least there were barracks already built for us to live in.

Those were the structures built by Ukrainians who were deported from their land some twenty years earlier as punishment for refusing to give up their properties and join the communal lives mandated by the communist regime. They were just dumped into the snow in the middle of a severe winter and told that if they wanted to have roofs over their heads, they had to build them themselves. There were plenty of trees around. They had very brutal conditions and not many of them were still alive when we arrived, just a handful of older folks. The drivers looked around at us and openly wondered how many of us would still be alive after 10 years. This was not encouraging.

By late afternoon we approached a group of wooden structures. This was to be our "home". There were six partitioned rooms in each structure. Each partition was meant to house one whole family. The end of the building was occupied by Ukrainians. We settled in one of the partitioned rooms. Sleeping accommodations were extremely primitive and consisted of boards elevated on makeshift saw horses. In the corner of the compartment there was a primitive clay stove filled with burning wood. The fire was started for us by the Ukrainians out of the goodness of their hearts. We were grateful. They were good people. The next morning, we were called to attend a general meeting. The camp commandant announced that this is where we will be living and working for the rest of our lives.

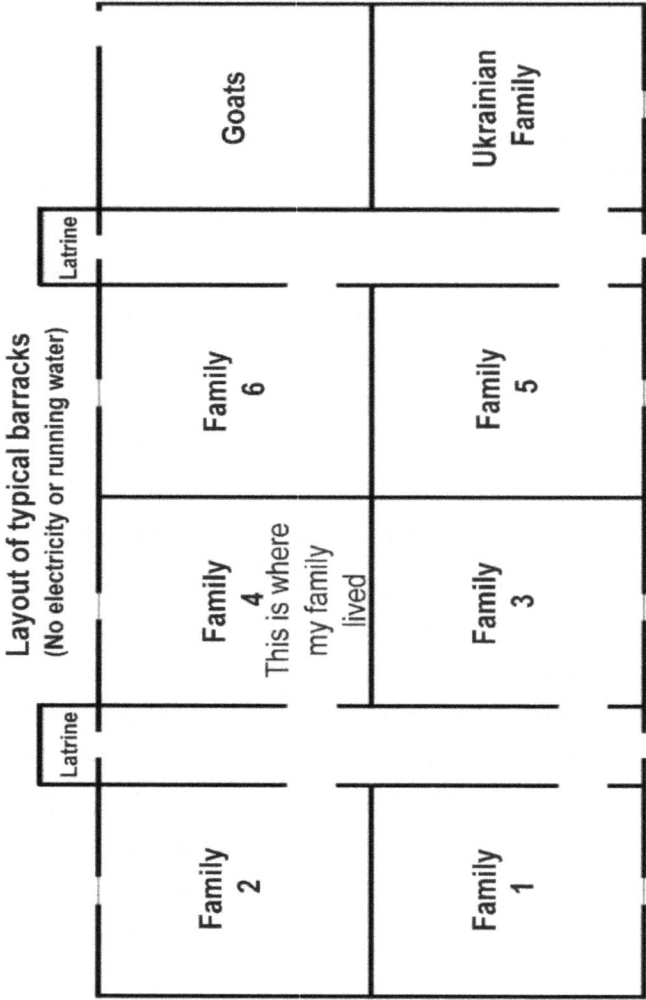

Layout of typical barracks
(No electricity or running water)

Latrine	Goats	
	Family 6	Ukrainian Family
	Family 4 This is where my family lived	Family 5
Latrine		Family 3
	Family 2	Family 1

All men and women age 15-65 were to report for work the next morning. This would give them the privilege to obtain 900 grams of bread and would allow their families to obtain 400 grams of bread per person daily. There was a saying in the Soviet Union; "those who do not work do not eat." This was not an empty slogan. This was enforced and was the reality of our lives. The allotted bread had to be paid for with money the workers would get according to what they would produce. There was a quota expected to be met by each worker every day. My mother, brother, and sister were of working age. My grandmother was 72 and I was 13 and neither of us had to work. All men, including my brother, were assigned to cut trees down and prepare the logs for hauling them to the river where they would be floated to the White Sea.

The pay was very low. People were simply not able to reach their required quotas, and so the pay was reduced according to what they produced. Conditions were brutal, demands from the foremen were extreme. Winter temperatures were down to 30-40 degrees Centigrade below zero or more. No one had proper clothing for such cold temperatures. The small allowance of bread and some watered-down soup was all we had to eat, and had to buy. It barely kept us alive. We were constantly hungry. Malnutrition and exhaustion were taking their toll. The men worked in the forests far from our camp so they stayed in even more primitive shacks during the week. My brother, being young and healthy, was taking it all quite well at first. He was trying to save some of his pay for us so we could buy our allowance of bread. He could come to see us once a week for one day. He looked more and more exhausted each time however.

My mother worked closer to our designated shack and could come to us every evening. The work was very hard for my mother. Not being used to such strenuous physical work, she struggled every day, crying in desperation. But she had to keep working. "No work and no food" as they said. She and other women were assigned to haul the logs loaded on primitive sleds pulled by half-starved and sick looking horses. The poor creatures were mistreated and undernourished just like the people and had no strength or will to work. My mother's horse was probably the weakest of them all. If she managed to get her sleds loaded early, she could place herself between other sleds and managed to get her horse to follow the others and she was ok. But most of the time she was stranded behind other sleds and her horse would not want to move. She would cry inconsolably, prompting him to get started and most of the time she was the last to get to the destination.

One time, it was already getting dark and she was left alone with her stubborn horse. There was no way she could get him to move in spite of her crying and pushing with all her strength. Luckily for her, along came an old local man who, seeing her all alone with the horse, stopped and said, "This horse is not used to your gentle and weak pleadings. This is the way to get him to move." He yelled at the horse using a lot of swear words, and sure enough the horse moved on, so my mother could finally join the other workers. The foreman, seeing that my mother was late most of the time and not producing enough for them, gave her a different job. It was hard physically but at least she did not have to deal with horses.

My sister, being 15 years old was lucky to be given a job as a mail delivery girl. Twice a week she went to a depot station, 8 miles away. The commandant would check all the mail and then let her deliver it to the people. People back in Poland, relatives and acquaintances of those here in Siberia who were lucky enough to have not been deported, found out where we were taken to and some correspondence that was strictly monitored and censored was permitted by our captors. We considered my sister to be very lucky to have this as a job. But to walk alone through a forest filled with wild animals in the snow with not a soul around, no doubt she was afraid. After some time, she got a break. The commandant, who was probably not a bad man, asked her what she was doing when in Poland. She said that she was attending a high school. Seeing her to be a smart girl, he said he would send her to the nearest high school so she could complete her studies. The nearest school was about 12 miles away, so she had to stay in a boarding house during the school year, coming to see us occasionally, when the school was out for a few days. I missed her but knew that she was better off at school.

I and other kids who were not of working age were to attend the local grade school with only up to the 5th grade available. Being at high school age at the time, all the boys and girls with me included were very reluctant to attend. We went but with open defiance and were not behaving very well. We were openly rebellious against communist propaganda which was fed to us daily. Defiantly, we were singing Polish hymns during class, refusing to speak Russian, and creating a hostile atmosphere. Of course, we were being foolish, not understanding the consequence this may bring, and just acting our age. But we carried on with an ignorant arrogance and belief that we were going back to our country soon and that gave us the courage to act like typical unruly teenagers. Unfortunately, the frustrated teacher, not being able to control us, finally reported us to authorities, and we got ourselves expelled and put on a duty list for work around the existing collective farm, without pay of course. We were given chores of cutting birch twigs for the goats, and later at spring time work in the fields, weeding, etc. It was hard to work on an empty stomach. We learned our lesson to obey.

When the long-awaited spring finally arrived, the spirits of the poor men working in the woods rose a bit. At least it got warmer. No more subzero weather. A reprieve from a very brutal winter. But with the warm temperature, another miserable plague appeared. Swarms of mosquitoes and tiny flies by the millions began to attack the poor workers. There was no way to escape them or prevent them from getting into their eyes, ears, nostrils, and mouths. The work had to go on no matter what. When hay time came, the younger and healthy men were sent to marsh lands to cut the hay. My brother was among them. The work was draining their strength to the limit. Their feet were always wet, wrapped with any available rugs, which never got dry. They had to wear them over and over until they could get back to camp and get some fresh rugs. My brother used to come to see us and he had horrible ulcers on his feet and his face was red and swollen from insect bites. He looked pitiful.

The life for all the rest of us in the camp, especially for the old people and infants was also very difficult. The "population" in a small cemetery up on a hill was steadily increasing. Infants born there died soon for lack of nourishment because mothers had nothing to feed them with and were malnourished themselves. The Soviet plan of liquidating us was working. I had the misfortune to perform a good deed in a tragic event that haunts me to this day. One young woman whom I knew, gave birth to a baby boy. She was very weak and unable to feed him and he died within a few days of being born. The woman's husband was working in the woods and was not allowed to come and help her bury her son. The neighbors made a small wooden coffin and my friend and I were asked to carry him to the cemetery. Holding the ends of two attached belts, we carried him, followed by the grieving mother and a small group of friends. Up on the hill, we stopped by a small opened grave. The poor mother was beyond comfort. She cried aloud and with her arms stretched up and pleaded, "Why would anyone let him die here, to be buried in this God-forsaken land?" It was heart breaking. I can still hear her helpless cry. There were many more deaths to come.

One of my friends, whose name was also Halina, was a prisoner at the camp with her father. Because of the tortuous working conditions, with time, her father became physically and mentally exhausted. One morning he could not even get up to go to work and stayed in bed. My friend and I went out to the woods to look for berries as usual. As we were heading back to the camp, someone ran towards us and turning towards my friend Halina said, "Your father died." My friend began to cry uncontrollably blaming herself for not being with him to help and letting him die alone. She ran back toward her barrack. My other friend and I walked slowly behind because we were overwhelmed and scared. We found out sometime later that our friend had ended up burying her father alone. She knew she had that responsibility and took it upon herself to accomplish it without asking for help. She isolated herself after that in a state of reverent mourning. After some time had passed, several weeks later, she began to accompany us again. She was like a completely different person, obviously changed by the whole ordeal. Forced to grow up and endure the tragedies of life and death in that terrible place. We could all see that the remorse from the loss of her father lingered on in her. The guilt of not being there for him weighed heavily on her heart. How does one forget? Now she had joined the hundreds of thousands of hearts wounded by the tragic loss of a loved one; cherished family members who had no strength to survive the brutal conditions of the Siberian labor camps. Unfortunately, her life had to go on but the pain lingered. I knew the feeling. For the rest of us living but barely surviving, the miserable struggle to live went on. We made ourselves believe that we would survive and someday would return to our homes in Poland. This faith kept us determined to persevere.

The hopeless and depressing days, which seemed to stretch out to nothingness, had a constant repeated theme; hungry to bed and hungry to rise. Unexpectedly, however, something happened that gave my family a short reprieve and a glimpse of hope. This was done by an older man living in our camp. He kept saying that he had a plan to escape. We were taking it lightly and with doubt. How could he accomplish it? But one day the news among the people broke out that the man was gone. Well, good luck to him we thought. He was gone for about three months, and as we predicted, was caught and came back escorted by armed soldiers. His plan did not work. He was apprehended and taken to another labor camp. But strangely, his misfortune gave my family a glimpse of my father's fate. When the man found himself among Polish prisoners at that camp, he told them that there are many families living where he escaped from. One man approached him, and giving his name, asked if by chance he heard the names of his family. This was my father. The returning prisoner said that the man looked old and was grey-haired. He lost all his teeth, tortured during interrogations. They demanded that he would sign a confession of his activities against the communist goals. He refused. The brutal and torturous questioning lasted for quite some time but to no avail. Finally, they sentenced him for not cooperating and being an enemy of the people, to the forced labor camp where our unfortunate escapee had found himself. My father spoke to him about his inquisition and torture in prison and gave him a small note for us and the man relayed it all when he was brought back to where we were. This was priceless news for us. My spirits were uplifted! My father was alive! There was hope that we will get to see him again. But, after a few lines of communication, everything stopped and we lost any trace of him again.

Rumors were constantly spreading quietly that Great Britain or America will hear about all of us. We certainly were not a small group of people, totaling well over a million and a half in number, spread throughout Siberia, so surely they will come to rescue us. The number of fortune tellers and dream interpreters who were fueling our hopes was growing. We never gave up the hope of returning to a free Poland. We also prayed secretly. This was not allowed in the communist country and could lead to deprivation of what little "freedom" and small portion of bread we had. There was a formidable structure called "the cold house", where people who were punished for any small insubordination, would be locked up for days without food and heat. This was another warning sign of speeding up the communist plan of liquidating us.

The first spring was coming to an end and a problem arose of what to do with the youngest school children while mothers were working. Rumors were spreading that they may be sent to an orphanage. That was frightening to all concerned. A meeting was called by the commandant. My grandmother, who for her age was healthy and full of energy, said she would be willing to take care of them all, provided that she would be given access to the school building, which was vacant for the summer, and food so she can feed them. The commandant agreed and showed her a storage filled with some food and told her that she can have as much as she can carry by herself. This was fine with my grandmother. On her own she hauled whatever was available like flour, potatoes, cereal, dry milk, and whatever she thought would be useful. She carried everything on her own back. She cooked meals, fed, and cared for all the children by herself. She made them take naps after eating, played games with them, and sang to them until their mothers could come and take them "home". My friends and I were not at an eligible age for this luxury. We kept sneaking by the school and peeking through the windows secretly so we saw it all. I was very proud of my grandmother. She never brought any scraps of food however because this could bring grave repercussions. I understood.

Despite the fact that we were prisoners, occasionally some of us children became adventurous as children normally did. Whatever free time we had left, we spent in the woods looking for berries. One very early Sunday morning, three of us girls and one other friend ventured to a new area near our camp in search of more blueberries. The place happened to be on the other side of the river. We were determined to get there somehow. Looking around, we saw a makeshift raft resting by the bank. We had no idea who owned it but decided to use it, vowing to return it when we were finished using it. We embarked on the vessel. Our friend found a sturdy looking pole resting near the bank and she decided that she was going to use it to get us to the other side of the river. About half way across however, she lost hold of the pole. We watched in horror as the raft floated away with the current and was carrying us close to a nearby dam. We had no control over the vessel. My friend yelled "Jump!" Everyone else jumped in and began to swim toward the bank that we came from. Obediently, I jumped in as well, but I could not swim. I hit the bottom, floated up, and then sank to the bottom again. My friends yelled to me to swim. In a state of panic, I flailed my arms and legs and somehow began to dog paddle but kept sinking again and again. Unexpectedly, all of a sudden, I felt the bottom with my feet and this time my head was above water. I was in shallow water. I pulled myself to the bank and, exhausted, collapsed into the arms of my friends. We were back on the same side of the river that we came from. We watched the raft go over the dam and out of sight. We kept our adventure to ourselves. I had nightmares for a long time because of it. I never did learn to swim and have no desire to do so.

We were hungry all the time and the berries that we went out to pick were a real blessing. We wanted to eat them all on the spot. However, our Ukrainian friends reminded us that we should start preserving them for the coming winter. "Summers are short here" they said. "Winters are very long so what are you going to eat then?" Reluctantly we began to save a good portion of berries for the winter. Somehow my family got hold of two wooden barrels in exchange for some of our clothing, which was very much in demand among local people. The berries, when crushed in the barrels, produced their own juice, fermented, and were edible when frozen in the winter. In time we gradually bartered as much of our clothing and bedding and whatever else we could spare for a little bit of potatoes from local people in the area. Eventually we were sleeping on our clothing, using jackets for a pillow. But even bartering did not come easy. My grandmother walked many miles in order to find people willing to share their food. Later on, in the summer, my friends and I learned about some mushrooms which I never heard about before, and if eaten fresh were rather toxic, but layered in the barrel with some salt and frozen, in the winter were edible. They had a terrible taste but were nutritious. We ate them and they helped keep us alive but they really did have a horrible taste.

Autumn was upon us bringing cold days. One day, I was alone. My grandmother was gone looking for people to trade some of our leftover belongings for some potatoes. The fire in our stove was going out and it was time to feed it. Outside of our barracks there was always some wood ready to be split for burning in the stove. I went outside. The axe was standing next to the pile of wood. I grabbed it and began to attempt to split some of the wood. Every attempt at splitting only resulted in either the axe bouncing off the log, or getting stuck in it. This was my first time I ever held an axe and I failed to chop even one silly piece of wood. I kept trying vigorously with all my strength but nothing worked. I kept trying in futility until all of my strength was spent. Exhausted, I straightened up, looked around, and to my horror saw three familiar boys walking slowly along the road towards me. Hoping that they did not see me, I dropped the axe and ran quickly inside hoping that they would keep walking away. After what seemed to be a safe time, I slowly ventured out, determined to master the art of using an axe. The boys were gone alright but to my shameful embarrassment I found a pile of split wood stacked neatly next to the axe ready to use in our stove. I was both furious with those boys and grateful for what they had done. How dare they notice my futile struggle? Now I would never live this down. I was sure they were having a great time by now laughing at my expense. Reluctantly, I picked up several of the split pieces of wood, went into the barracks, and fed the stove. My grandmother upon her return was pleased to see the fire going. She did not ask any questions. I tried my best to avoid seeing the three boys after that knowing they would make fun of me. To my surprise, when we met later on, they made no remarks and acted as if nothing ever happened. I kept quiet about it and so did they. It was very generous and mature of them.

The extremely short summer of 1940 passed and winter was upon us again. People around me were noticeably weaker and sick. The workers, half starved and trying to reach the required norm at work began to die. Very often, right there at work. With no time allowed to bury them, they were left in the snow, casually sometimes covered by passing co-workers with a couple of branches, left to remain there forever. Work had to continue. Nothing else mattered to the regime. More and more people died as the cold brutal winter raged. We had been there over one year already.

There was a change in the administration towards the end of the winter in 1941. The camp commandant, who was very strict but showed some humane qualities of understanding occasionally, was replaced by someone who was quite opposite in nature. The new commandant had frequent fits of fury and showed no mercy to anyone. His protruding eyes were enough to freeze anyone in terror. We gave him the nickname 'Furious Eyes".

The signs of spring of 1941 were approaching. There were four of us girls who constantly were in search of anything to eat. So now we were spending most of our days looking for berries called lingonberries, which having survived the winter, were beginning to show up on the sunny slopes of small hills from under the snow. They were quite tasty although never enough to calm the hunger pains. Everyone's constant focus was on food and how to get it. That was the way the communist plan was working. Do not think about trying to revolt, just concentrate on what to eat and how to survive. But this did not quite work with us. The thought of being released from that God-forsaken regime and returning to our homes sustained us and gave us strength to go on. Still, malnutrition was taking its toll on us. All kinds of illnesses were invading us. Scurvy was rampant. I had ulcers on both of my legs that would not heal.

Early during the slowly developing spring, my family got the chance of obtaining something that was virtually impossible for anyone to obtain. Our neighbor, the Ukrainian woman was working at a nearby dairy collective farm. Seeing my miserable condition, she told my mother in secret, that she should send me early some prearranged morning to where the woman worked some 4 miles away where she would let me get some skimmed milk which sometimes was left over. This would be a one-time chance and no one was to know about it. So, on a morning designated by her, I ventured out holding our tea kettle in my hand. It was still dark and cold. I was walking along the river. There was no road to speak of, just some planks laid down across the wet and muddy pathway. It was passable but very slippery. I got to the milk house safely, watching for the little window to be opened which was to be my signal to get closer. She opened the window and signaled to me. I came over to the window and gave her my kettle, which she quickly filled and then closed the window. I retreated in haste and proceeded back to our shack, being careful not to be seen by anyone. When out of the danger zone, I breathed a sigh of relief and felt happy and excited at the thought of being able to provide my family with the precious milk which, maybe with some potatoes, would be quite a feast for us. We would not go to bed hungry that night I thought. As I walked, I heard a soft chiming sound behind me. There was a man riding on a sled pulled by a horse. The old man slowed down and I stepped aside to let him pass. I was not afraid of him. He waved to me and said in a friendly

voice in Russian, "Be careful, it is slippery." "Yes" I
responded and a few moments after he passed, I slipped
on a plank and fell down on my back and my
outstretched arms hit the frozen ground. I looked at my
hand still holding the kettle, and to my horror, I saw the
precious milk spilling out onto the ground. I got up and
looked inside. There was no milk left! None at all! I
began to cry aloud almost running back home. It did not
matter anymore if anyone saw me or heard me cry at
the camp. Weeping bitterly, I went inside our room
where my grandmother was waiting for me. Seeing me
enter crying she took the empty kettle, hugged me, and
holding me in her arms she said, "Now, now child,
don't cry over the spilled milk." I still cannot bear to
hear those words said casually. I never mentioned my
unfortunate expedition to the group of my friends and
our mundane life continued with searching for berries.

A little later that spring my friends and I got a
message from the workers. This was again both
challenging and hopeful. They said that during the last
few weeks, their cook was treating them once a week to
some kind of crude pancakes. My daring brother said
that if we would get permission from 'Furious Eyes" to
get to their eating place on a given day, the cook would
surely let us have some pancakes to eat. We would have
to arrive there at the right time on a particular day. This
was again a special secret message. The four of us
brave girls went to the commandant's office that day in
the morning and meekly asked if we could go and visit

our working men. Since they couldn't come to the camp for several weeks, they needed some extra clothing. To our amazement he let us go. We hastened to get there at the right time. The place was a few miles away. The trip paid off. After the workers were given their portions, the cook gave each one of us a few of the pancakes. They were not of course, what one would call regular size pancakes, but as little as they were, they provided something warm and solid to eat. They were delicious. So, the following week, we decided to try the same trick again. But it did not work. The commandant looked at us with his furious eyes and yelled, "I know what this is about and if you come here once more with your story, I will lock you up in the cold hut, so out with you!" We turned around and ran for our lives. That was the end of our pancakes.

There was one incident when this commandant appeared to be quite a different individual. During the month of May, my family and some of our friends began to gather in our room once weekly for our traditional May devotions. We had a large icon of the Virgin Mary which my grandmother managed to smuggle along. It was hanging on a wall in our room at all times, although displaying of any religious items even in the privacy of one's own room was strictly forbidden in that country and could bring harsh consequences. We felt quite confident that no one would even think of reporting this to the authorities. But we were wrong. One evening, when we prayed kneeling, the door suddenly was pushed open loudly and in came "Furious Eyes" the commandant. We were frozen in fright still kneeling. He looked around and fixing his stare at the picture, he barked, "Whose is this?" There was dead silence for a moment, after which my brother, who was with us for his day off said calmly, "It is ours." With my heart pounding fiercely, I thought to myself, well now he is going to arrest my brother and he will most likely share my father's fate. But an incredible thing happened. This seemingly unfeeling and cruel man looked at us as we kneeled and just said, "This is forbidden." To our disbelief, he quietly walked to the door and softly closed it behind him. We were quite understandingly in shock! A man known to be cruel and almost without mercy to those who would even slightly deviate from his rules would act completely differently and did nothing? Our friends went home in fright and stopped coming for prayers, but we continued to pray. I could not stop thinking about the incident. Why did he not react in his usual way? Why? Did our praying group for an instance bring some memories from his past? Did this by some chance remind him about his parents, and could it be that he witnessed a similar happening in the past and consequences which followed? Was the demeanor that caused us to give him that nickname a part of him because of what he saw that happened to his parents? Many children in the Soviet Union saw atrocities unleashed on their own parents by the communists.

This stayed on my mind for quite a while and taught me another lesson. Never judge anyone by their appearance and actions. One does not know what may have triggered their demeanor, and way of life.

In June of 1941, we heard news that the German Army attacked the Soviet Union, their allies in crime. Both were our enemies and we did not care what the outcome of this would be. But our Ukrainian friends were hoping that the Germans would win and that may make it possible for them to return to their land in the Ukraine. We did not share their hopes. Most likely the Germans would have them all shot as well as us too. But the Germans were moving east pretty quickly and obviously the Soviets needed help to stop them. The next thing we heard was that the British government, together with the Polish government in London signed a treaty with the Soviet government. This meant amnesty for all of us in the labor camps. Under the agreement, all Polish men deported to labor camps in the Soviet Union were to be released and allowed to join the Polish Army in the Soviet Union but under British command. Their families were to be released also, and remain under British protection, together with the Polish government in exile. This was absolutely too good to believe but it was true. We were free at last, although not able to return home quite yet. The war was raging on but when this was all over, we would surely be going home. For now, the men had to reach the point where the army was being formed. At the time however, we did not know how to reach that point. Soviet authorities did not want to give out much information. They had other plans for us. They wanted to incorporate all Polish men within the Soviet Army, not under British command.

The Polish government formed special delegate points throughout the Soviet Union and from them people found out that the army was being formed far to the south and east, close to the Afghanistan border. The poor men from our camp began to leave and head for the far southeast. We did not hear from or about them, except in one case where one man was found dead in the woods close to the train station. Exhausted and hungry he could not make it very far. His 17-year-old daughter went over and pulling a small sled, brought his body to our camp. This prompted the people to send two men to the nearest delegate point near Archangelsk to learn what we, the rest of us should do. They advised us to stay put together for awhile rather than to try to get to the Polish Army individually on our own. Being completely exhausted from the inhumane treatment and hunger, we would surely perish on our way. They told our two delegates that if we stayed together as a fairly large group, they would demand that a train be sent for us all and take us to our destination near the far southeastern border. So, we waited.

Winter came upon us and we were still there. The situation was becoming quite desperate. With no work, there was no pay and no money to buy much smaller portions of bread. There was almost nothing to eat. We existed literally according to their slogan; "No work, no food". My mother was sharing the remaining content of our barrels which I filled with lingonberries and mushrooms, with whoever came asking for help. She could not refuse anyone although she knew that soon we would be left with nothing to eat ourselves.

That winter was a culmination of our struggle to survive, but for so many people, futile. Our camp looked like a ghost town. People remained inside of their rooms in complete lethargy, hardly able to move. Weak and hungry, we patiently waited for the promised train which was to come and get us out of that God-forsaken land. It finally came. On February 10, 1942, strangely, exactly two years after our deportation, we were informed that the train will be waiting for us at a depot some 12 miles away. To our amazement, the camp administration even provided two big tractors with platforms for us powered by wood blocks that our people had to chop for the two long years. This was the only way to run any engine in the below-zero temperatures in Siberia. So whatever belongings we were left with, we loaded on the tractors and with a sigh of relief, left the camp. Our Ukrainian friends however, were calling us traitors for siding with the Soviets at the time. We felt sorry for them but could not help but leave them behind. They were Soviet citizens, we were not.

It was very cold on the way to the depot and almost impossible to ride on the tractors motionless so I tried to walk most of the way behind the tractors, which were moving very slowly. We reached the depot in the dark of evening and unfortunately did not see any train. It was not there. The man in charge of the depot said that most likely it will arrive by morning. This was very bad news. We were facing a very brutal winter night out in the open. My family however was in luck. The depot was in the town where my sister was attending school. She had a very good friend who lived there, so my sister ran to their home and told her friend about our situation. Her family welcomed us into their home for the night. We were also able to bring along two other families. Their house was very small but they did not mind the inconvenience so we gratefully rested down on the floor, relieved to be in a warm room. The girl's mother even made some potato soup which we devoured thankfully. My grandmother, wanting to repay them somehow for their hospitality, said that maybe she could do some knitting for them and having been provided with an old sweater, she ripped it and proceeded to knit a pair of gloves. She was a speedy knitter. I slept all night. My brother and another man took turns checking on the train.

By morning the train arrived. It was a freight train of course. A number of people did not make it to see it. They were too weak to survive. The cold night and hunger took its toll. We managed to get up inside the train. The setup was familiar, the same as the train they brought us to Siberia on except no soldiers. My family got situated on an upper deck and soon the train started to move. It was very cold inside but the sound of the moving train was calming. We were moving forward to freedom.

The feeling did not last very long however. On the first night of our trip we woke up to a strange silence. The train was not moving. Someone looked through the little opening on the side and said that we were in the middle of nowhere. There was no station or any buildings around us. Then someone from the front of the train remarked that the engine was gone. We were obviously abandoned. The whole day passed. We stood still, left on a side track. Later on, that afternoon, we started noticing lights in the distance. Clearly, there had to be a village of some kind. My brother, sister and I decided to start walking toward those lights and those who could walk joined us. Surely if there are people, they would give us something to eat. Holding each other's hands, we struggled through the knee-deep snow. As we approached the village, we noticed a large building and we could definitely smell food. We saw groups of people leaving the building. We walked in and asked the cook if we could have something to eat. She said they were ready to close down but having some soup left over, told us to get bowls and stand in line. Those in front got their soup no problem. My sister and I were also lucky to get our bowls filled, but they ran out before my brother got to the end. He was already swollen from malnutrition. We gave him one of our bowls of soup and we both shared the other one. Tears were streaming down my brother's swollen face as he was drinking the hot soup. He said quietly, "Thank you." At least we warmed our stomachs to perk us up for a while. We struggled back to the train, unfortunately without anything for those who stayed behind.

Night came and I guess I must have fallen asleep. I suddenly woke up feeling a sharp jerk. Our train began to move again. It was going fast and in the right direction. We arrived at Vologda station where some members of our Polish delegation greeted us. They were expecting us somewhat sooner and I think they "persuaded" local officials to get our train to move toward the right destination. We were just lucky. Obviously, the Soviets were trying to make it hard for us to reach our freedom and join the Polish Army down south. After all, we were not deported from our homes just to work for them and survive, but to work and perish.

The train, now moving rather fast, was heading southeast, away from Moscow, and then further to the southeast, all the way to Alma Ata, in the Kazakhstan Province, close to the Chinese border. We were just a "drop in the ocean" among the crowds of people who had already reached that point. I couldn't help but to think that here there are 500,000 people who survived the labor camps and lived to hear about amnesty, but what happened to the rest of the more than one million people deported from eastern Poland? Thousands of men perished, forced to work in inhumane conditions. Thousands of mothers died leaving their children as orphans, and also thousands of women became so to speak, "orphaned mothers", by having to bury their children in that hostile land. The system worked well according to the Soviet plan. I am not pointing my finger at anyone. They were the product of a Godless ideology which showed its face in many forms. In this case, the plan was to exterminate all Polish people deported from the eastern part of Poland. No need for gas chambers like the Nazis. Why bother. The vast Siberian land took care of their plan very well. Behind the trees, under the snow, scattered over the vast steppes, the Angel of Death had its fill, and then some.

Around 500,000 survivors headed for freedom, trying to reach the far southeastern Soviet Union where the Polish Army under British command was being formed. This was a great 'Exodus" of poor deportees escaping from Soviet slavery. Having no means of traveling in regular fashion, they walked on foot, rode in buggies provided by sympathizers, smuggled themselves on or under a train, they took advantage of everything that could bring them closer to freedom. About 300,000 managed to reach their goal but about 200,000 did not make it. Most families had to resettle for the period of waiting while our government was negotiating with other countries to receive us even temporarily, just so we were out of the reach of the Soviets.

We stayed on the train all that time. There were no immediate plans for us. However, our numbers were slowly decreasing. Delegated nurses were checking us out trying to help during this situation. All kinds of diseases were beginning to spread. My mother and sister were ok. My brother was quite swollen and had a case of night blindness caused by vitamin deficiency. My grandmother and I however were very sick. Because of a rather high fever, the nurse recommended that I should go to a hospital, fearing that my illness may be contagious. So, they put me on a small two-wheeled cart pulled by a donkey and with my mother beside me, I was taken to a hospital. After a good and well needed bath, my lice infested head was shaved and I was placed in a large ward filled with women suffering from all sorts of illnesses. High fever kept me in a semi-conscious state. Some broth and crackers were brought to my bedside but I was too ill to eat so I let a woman next to me take it, which she did and ate it all hastily and replaced the empty bowl by my bedside.

My mother came to visit me again bringing good news that Persia (now Iran) agreed to accept us all, at least for the time being. Our train and gradually the rest of the people were to be transported to Krasnovodsk, a port city by the Caspian Sea, and from there we were to sail over to the Persian side. This was good news but she said that I may have to stay behind because I still had a very high fever and the doctor refused to release me. She had talked to the Polish Relief Organization, who promised to take care of me. I did not care, being as sick as I was but my mother was very worried. There were already thousands of orphaned children under their care, and she did not want to leave me behind. The good doctor told her to come back the next morning and if my fever goes down a bit, he would release me.

The next morning my mother returned and since my fever did go down somewhat the doctor said I could be released. There was no ride provided this time and I had to walk all the way to the train. I don't know how far the train was, but this was the longest walk of my life. I was able to make a few steps at a time and then would collapse to the ground to rest. This went on and I thought it would never end and I would never get there. Exhausted, I pleaded with my mother to just leave me there so I could rest on a rock and lie there forever. There was no strength in me at all or will to make another step. She was pleading with me to go on, supporting my weak body as much as she could, given that she was not very strong herself. I leaned on her and she almost dragged me the rest of the way. Finally, we reached the train. Several people were standing by the entry to the train, prompting us to move faster, saying the train was going to start moving very soon. When we got close enough, they hoisted me up into the train. My mother followed and I fainted on the floor. The train began to move shortly after.

The train finally reached Krasnovodsk where after we took showers, they loaded us on a freight ship. We were packed like sardines. There was standing room only. Our government wanted to get as many people as quickly as possible out of harm's way. They did not trust the Soviets.

My grandmother and I collapsed on the deck, not caring if people would step over or on us. We were too weak to stand. Someone in uniform bent over my grandmother and she cried in disbelief, "Is that you Olek?" Olek was her oldest son and an army officer who was deported separately to a different part of the Soviet Union. After amnesty he made his way to this same place and was put on this ship and, like other army officers, was given his own cabin. He got the two of us up and brought us to his cabin. Another merciful help in my life. When we reached Pahlevi on the Persian side, people felt relieved. Free at last!

We were still a long way from our homes but people didn't seem to mind now. They thought that somehow and maybe soon all of us would be returning to Poland. My grandmother and I however, two skeletons on the verge of death, did not feel anything. There was a lot of food now but we were beyond feeling hungry. It was hard for me to swallow any kind of food. There were many sick people like us of course and they felt the same. My brother joined the army, led by hand by my

mother to be enlisted. He was still affected by the
blinding sickness. From Pahlevi we were transported on
very comfortable coaches to Qazvin and then to Tehran.
The city looked very modern and large. We stopped at
its outskirts so they could situate us in different spots.
Healthy people were placed in two camps and sick
people in hundreds of tents that made up an emergency
field hospital. My grandmother and I were separated
and placed in different tents. I don't remember this
happening myself but was told about it later. I was in a
semi-conscious state at that time and running a high
fever again. Probably after many days had passed, I was
awakened to people around me crying and moaning in
agony. One woman, a pool of blood by her bed, cried
"Please finish me off. Just kill me." She was in agony
and just moments later she died. The nurse's aides
carried her out on a stretcher. Soon after, another
woman was carried out, also dead. Everyone around me
seemed to be in agony and dying. I panicked and began
to cry thinking that my turn will come soon. And where
was my mother? What is going on here? No one paid
attention to me. The doorway to the tent was pulled out
open and I could see people passing by, so hoping that
maybe my mother will appear, I kept my eyes fixed on
the opening.

My head was pounding and I felt very weak. I guess
miracles do happen for after a while, I did see my
mother passing by. I cried with all the strength I could
gather, "Mama!" but she kept on walking and

disappeared from my sight. My heart sank. This is it I thought, I will surely die here. But she did hear someone cry mama so she stopped, walked back hoping to help someone somehow. I saw her again and thought I yelled this time, "Mama, this is me, Hala." She was not allowed to enter because this was a tent for people with tuberculosis. She just cried to me not to worry, she would be back.

My mother told me this part of the story later on. As soon as she and my sister were settled in the camp, she rushed to the hospital area to look for me and my grandmother. She went to the nurse's station asking how to find us in that sea of tents. The nurse gave her a long list of names to go through and look for our names. If we were on the list that meant that we were dead. She found my grandmother's name. It simply said "typhoid". That was all. After all the good she had done in Siberia, taking care of the children, leading us in prayer, and being a great support for us, she just became a statistic. She was one out of 200,000 sick people who died in that hospital from different kinds of disease that they contracted during their miserable life in Siberia. My name was not on the list. So, my mother started walking through the long rows of tents, reading the names. I was placed in the tuberculosis tent so she did not even stop to read the names, knowing that I did not have TB. That was when I saw her and called to her.

She ran quickly back to the nurse's station, found the doctor, and said that I was in the TB area and she knows for sure that I did not have the disease and would the doctor please come and examine me. The good doctor, as busy as she was, followed my mother to my tent, examined me, listened to my lungs, and immediately ordered to have me removed from there and placed in the convalescent ward. They treated me for some kind of malaria typical for that part of the Soviet Union in Asia and after a few weeks, they released me from the hospital. I walked out wearing some kind of hospital clothing and heavy socks for lack of shoes. It seemed like a long walk and I was still quite weak but it was a far cry from my exhausting walk back in Alma Ata. Holding my mother's hand, I arrived in a healthy part of camp.

My ordeal was not over however. Back in camp, there was a lot of food, normal food, but it was too rich for my weakened stomach and I came down with a very bad case of dysentery in its extreme form. I was very sick again. We were rather cramped in a primitive military building and women close to us were concerned that I would get them all sick so I should go back to the hospital. Someone came up with what she thought was the only solution to my problem. She suggested that a shot of whiskey mixed with ground pepper will cure me. She said that it never fails. My mother did not like the idea but women who were convinced it would work brought the drink over and, hovering around me, prompted me to drink it. Not wanting to go back to the hospital, I drank it fast. It filled me with burning fire! I could hardly breathe and collapsed immediately. But after a few minutes I began to feel better and sat up to everyone's relief. Obviously, it helped. All the bad symptoms slowly left me and I was back among the living. The nurse prescribed a special diet and I was regaining my strength. Even my hair began to grow back.

Persia was very friendly and sympathetic toward us but really could not let us stay too much longer. They simply were not prepared to accommodate such a great number of people. Statistically, out of 500,000 who survived the labor camps in the Soviet Union, 200,000 still died on the way to freedom and in the hospital in Tehran so we were among the 300,000 who were living in Persia. We had to be relocated to other countries willing to take us for a longer duration, and after some negotiations the problem was resolved. The newly formed Polish Army under British command was shipped to Iraq. Richard, my brother, wearing his new army uniform came to say goodbye to us. It was great to see him back to his normal cheerful self. He was in a great mood, proud to belong to the Polish Army. He looked forward to a bright future for all of us when we would meet again in our home country. Cheerfully, he graciously hugged all of us, saluted us, turned around, and marched away. I never saw him again.

As for the rest of us civilian families and thousands of orphans, we were accepted by Mexico, Lebanon, New Zealand, and British colonies in Africa. My mother, my sister, and I were designated to settle in what is presently called Tanzania, Africa. This was pretty far from our home but the war was still going on so it seemed ok to spend the final episode, as we all believed, in an exotic country like Africa. We were to be under British protection. On August 1, 1942 we began our long journey to Africa. First by train to the Persian Gulf, then on a ship to Karachi, India where we disembarked and stayed for about a month, then finally on another ship all the way to Tanzania, East Africa where we lived for seven years. My Siberian experience was over but not forgotten.

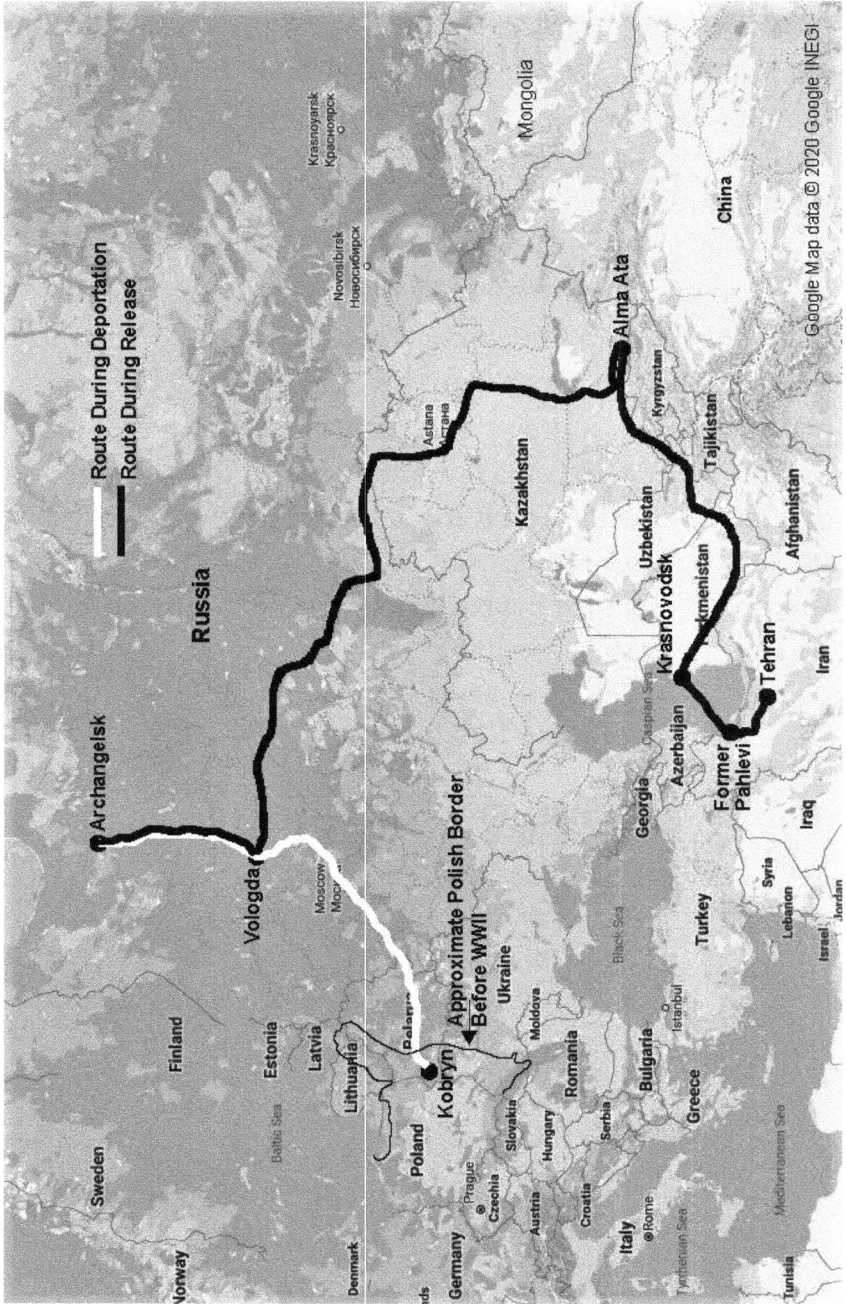

EPILOGUE

During our stay in Africa, the dream of returning to our homes never ceased. But what ended it was a historical event which changed the lives of millions of Polish people. In May of 1945 there was a meeting between Churchill, Stalin, and Roosevelt in Yalta. The end result was tragic for us. The entire eastern part of Poland was to become a part of the Soviet Union permanently. That is where we lived before deportation. We lost our home and could never go back there – ever. There were also more tragic events in my life in Africa. My sister, who back in Siberia became very ill after one of her walks from school to our camp, had rheumatic fever which, untreated, became heart disease and the African climate caused her heart to fail. She died at the age of 19. My brother, serving in the Polish Army, had joined a special paratroop unit and on his first mission to jump into Poland during the underground war, his plane was shot down by the Germans. The whole crew was killed. My brother was buried in a military cemetery in Poland after the war.

The fate of my uncle, the man who came to see us when we were on the train about to be deported is another tragedy of this story. When the Nazis attacked the Soviets in 1941 and violated the pact between the two powers, they began pushing east through the eastern part of Poland. They eventually conquered Kobryn, the town where we were arrested in and also where my uncle lived. He joined the Polish underground to fight the Nazis but unfortunately, he and other members was eventually caught. They were forced at gunpoint to dig a large ditch, were lined up in front of it after completing it, and then executed. Their bodies fell into the very grave that they were forced to dig for themselves. When the Nazis subsequently withdrew from town, my aunt as well as other survivors exhumed the bodies of their loved ones. She was able to give him a decent burial in the Catholic cemetery in Kobryn. She managed to stay in Kobryn where she took care of my uncle's grave until her own death. These events were relayed to me by my mother-in-law who lived in Kobryn throughout the war and knew my aunt. We moved my mother-in-law to the United States after the war where she stayed with us until her death in the 1970s.

After seven years in Africa and four years after the end of the war, my mother and I relocated to England. There, in London, I met a Polish officer, my future husband. He had a visa to settle in America and in May of 1950, he sailed for New York. After settling down in Chicago, he proposed to me by mail, paid for mine and my mother's passage on the Queen Mary, first class, and we arrived in the United States in December. In February of 1951 we were married. We had two sons, Thomas and Richard. Twenty years later we moved to

Wisconsin and settled down permanently. My mother lived with us and passed away in 1994 at the age of 98. It is now 2020 and I am still here, living at my American home in Wisconsin. I am 93 years old now and recently greeted the arrival of my fourth great-grandchild. But after all these years, there is still a grain of pain and nostalgia in my heart. It is still there because I and my family did not leave our home willingly. We were not some refugees looking for a better life elsewhere. We were happy there, thank you, but we were forced out by the armed Soviet soldiers. Our home was confiscated and we were deported to Siberia. And now, if I were to go back to my family home I would be, putting it mildly – an intruder.

Monument to Poles who died and are buried in Tehran.

Some of the many graves of those whose journey ended in Tehran.

My Mother and I at my sister's grave in Africa.

My mother and I in Africa.

Me in Nairobi, Kenya during a scouting seminar.

Me in front of our home in Africa.

Me at the grave of my brother in Poland many years later.

These medals were awarded to my brother posthumously. They were delivered and presented to my mother in the 1980s by a special envoy sent by the Polish Government in London when they found out that his mother was still alive.

My dear father in the prime of his life.

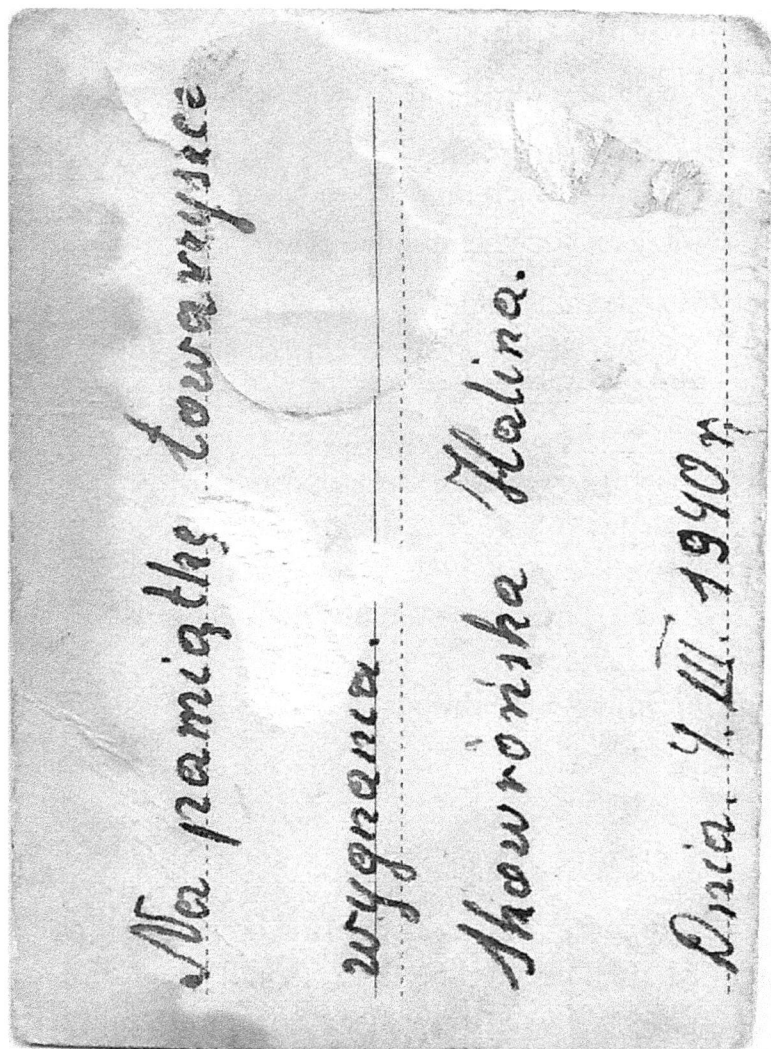

The back of the cover photo with my writing on it.
It says: "As a memory for a companion in deportation".

My Family in the United States

Tadeusz Jaworski – Husband – deceased

Thomas Jaworski – Son
Cathy Sweeney – Mother of Sonia
 Sonia Jaworski – Granddaughter

Richard Jaworski – Son
Heidi Soergel – Mother of Roger, Jessica, and Brian
 Roger Jaworski – Grandson
 Alicia Jaworski – Granddaughter-in-law
  Joseph Jaworski – Great-Grandson
  Ana Jaworski – Great-Granddaughter
  Arwen Jaworski – Great-Granddaughter
  Amelé Jaworski – Great-Granddaughter
 Jessica Jaworski – Granddaughter
 Brian Jaworski – Grandson

Afterword

My grandmother managed to bring some photographs with her to Siberia in a small box. While we were there, a friend of my sister's wanted a photo of her as a memento. We had no photographs of my sister but we had one of me and I asked her if she would like that. She welcomed the offer. That is the photograph on the cover of this memoir. I was about eight years old when it was taken. Before giving it to her I wrote a dedication to her as a companion in deportation.

When we arrived in Pahlevi the officials there confiscated everything we had and burned it all in fear of spreading more disease through those items. I met this same friend of my sister's ten years later in London. She still had the photograph with her. I don't know how she managed to smuggle it through but she did. She offered it back to me and I accepted it.

The photographs of my sister were taken in Africa. The photographs of my father were given to me by a close relative who managed to stay in Poland through the war. The photograph of my brother was sent to my mother by the Polish Government in exile in London after she had already come to the United States.

Halina Jaworski

www.ingramcontent.com/pod-product-compliance
Lightning Source LLC
Chambersburg PA
CBHW071639040426
42452CB00009B/1695